To Pa

Thank you so much
for being there for me!
6 months ago you told
me I was in a wilderness
time in my life, I have
walked through it, And
God has brought me to
my greater!

Walk in purpose,
LIVE on purpose!
Thank you!

Love you,

DANGERS OF THE MIND

The Distractions That Can Kill Your Dreams!

When you place actions behind your intentions, you can be UNSTOPPABLE!

Unless otherwise noted, all Scripture quotations are from the New International Version (NIV) Bible Copyright © 1984, by International Bible Society. Zondervan Corporation.

Dangers of the Mind by Kristen Hopkins

Copyright © 2014 by
Kristen Hopkins
Principal, Chief Creative Officer
KH II Public Relations | PO Box 54406
Atlanta GA, 30308
www.kh2pr.com

Library of Congress Control Number: 2014910828
International Standard Book Number: 9780692238257

A word to readers of...

Dangers of the Mind

This book is dedicated to anyone who has birthed a vision but has allowed distraction, procrastination, or what they perceive as the lack of progress to delay its manifestation. Before long they find themselves simply stuck in a rut of despair feeling like an unfulfilled, abandoned failure.

Your most vulnerable place of attack is your thought life. This includes your hopes, loves, fears, and most especially your dreams! How does this happen? We look away from our dreams and all of the good things happening in our lives and look toward a big stack of lies, misdirection and misinformation which serve only to curtail and even derail our vision.

Prayerfully, after reading this book you will gain insight on the common dangers you may encounter against your *"thought life."* This knowledge is critical because you must change your way of thinking in order to get a clear vision of your future -- the destiny God has for *you*! This is not about getting more stuff, becoming more important or being more connected. It is **always** about realizing your greater purpose by harnessing the power of our thoughts. We must prepare to expand our thinking in order to change our mind about what we see, think, hear and do. So let's ready our hearts and minds to dive in and see what is in store for us!

Keep Believing!

An avid Dreamer!

This book is dedicated in loving memory of my aunt

Gwendolyn Stoval.

I never got to say goodbye, so this is for you!

Acknowledgements

First of all, I'd like to thank God who has been my comforter, best friend, provider, and way maker. He has put this book into my heart and I just followed His lead, so I am nothing without him.

Next I would like to thank my mother Sharon Hopkins Wilson, who has ALWAYS supported me in everything that I do. Mom, you are my rock and you mean the world to me.

I would also like to thank my immediate family and friends. Especially, my dad Woodrow Wilson, my sister Ashley Hopkins, my grandparents in North Carolina (Daisy and Jerry Chandler) and my Grandmother in CT, Geraldine Findley. You typically don't hear of women writing a book about their personal life journey at 26 years of age; but so many of you are just as excited about this effort as I am. I so appreciate your ongoing support and encouragement!

I would personally like to thank one of my best friends and business partner, Katrina Highsmith, for always supporting my ideas and cheering me on.

This book would not be possible without a team of people that has helped me through this process. I would like to thank my editor, Valdenia Simmons and her company VisionWorks Consulting. She has amazed me over the months of knowing her, her brilliant ideas, exceptional editing skills, and how she has brought my vision to life. Dr. Faith C. Wokoma has personally helped me in my life. She is a life coach and an amazing woman of God. Thank you for reading this book, and writing my foreward! I would like to thank Tambria Kemp with Blu Kolla Designs for the book cover and Jamal Simmons with Frame 88 Studios for the photography.

Lastly, I would like to thank you, the people that support me by purchasing this book. You're in for a treat!

Dangers of the Mind

Table of Contents

Foreword

Everything we see around us exists because someone thought of it, followed through, persevered, endured failure, and tried again. The mind is the place where ideas are born but also where they can die. The mind is the place that declares, "You can conquer the world" and in the same breath say "never mind, just give up!" In the Scriptures, the terms "mind" and "heart" are used interchangeably. One that comes to mind is found in Proverbs 4:23, "Guard your heart above all else, for it is the source of life" (HCSB).

So what happens when you do not guard your mind? It becomes occupied with dangerous thoughts like fear, doubt, procrastination, false perceptions and negative beliefs. Slowly they begin to storm your mind and soon they rule your world. We must learn how to guard our mind so that it becomes life-giving and world changing and you cannot change the world if you are constantly in a battle with your thought life!

Another scripture tells us to "be transformed by the renewing of your mind..." (Romans 12:2, HCSB). The key word is *renewing* which indicates that transformation takes place not just once, but on a consistent basis. We start by aligning it with positive thoughts that are true, good, praiseworthy, uplifting and motivating. We cannot allow our negative experiences, trials and traumas to influence our decision-making. When that happens we slowly surrender the hope in our lives and as hope dwindles we become disillusioned which then gives way to inactivity.

Kristen does a tremendous job of identifying the dangerous thoughts -- if left unchecked can cause your life to navigate on a course that you could have never imagined. Kristen offers clear step by step directions on how to take control of your journey to get to the place you desire. In order for a lie to lose its power, it must be challenged and replaced with the truth! This book offers a candid look at a young woman's journey to bring all of the elements that make up your thought life into proper perspective.

You were made for something extraordinary. Now that this book is in your hands allow it to help you identify and examine the dangerous thoughts in your life. You will never be the same again. So sit back and enjoy the book. Take the time to assess and challenge those thoughts that are contrary to who you are and who you know that you were born to be. Read this book and begin to dream again!

Faith C. Wokoma, Psy.D.

Dangers of the Mind

The Journal

My hope is that as you read this book its lessons will help you avoid the dangerous thinking that can lead to powerless living. One effective way to integrate new thinking and behaviors into our lives is by journaling. There are journal exercises at the end of each chapter. There are 3 benefits to journaling:

1. It will assist you in developing a plan of action for bringing your vision to reality.
2. It helps you to clarify your preferred future by putting your vision to paper. This is very powerful.
3. It helps you to actively bring your vision to reality by identifying your short- and long-term goals and objectives.

If you take the time to walk through the exercises following each chapter, you will find that it helps you to apply the lessons learned to your life.

Chapter 1

Dangers of the Mind

Let's take a moment of silence. I mean REAL silence. Eliminate any and all noise, no matter the source and just sit in total silence. As I explained in the opening, you must prepare to expand your thinking in order to change your mind about what you see, think, hear and do. So let's understand that noise is more than an audible distraction. It is anything that blocks you from sending, receiving or understanding a message. So let's begin by turning off the television, music, technology, family, friends and most especially your phone! Sounds easy enough? Now comes the hard part.

How long is it before the noise in your mind takes over? Can you keep your mind from wandering off to some task, conversation or person? The average person can only engage in total silence for a few minutes. Basically, there is some form of "internal" noise going off in our heads all day long. Often times we forget that our thoughts play an important role in making us who we are in life and are often the factor that determines the level of success or failure we attain in our future. Left unchecked, our thoughts can be one of our most powerful assets or the source of our greatest threats. Yes, our thoughts can be dangerous.

Picture yourself walking into a board meeting of co-workers, business partners, or clients. What if for today and today only, you could tap into each person's thoughts? What type of thoughts might you come across? Now think about if someone could do this to you? Not so fun anymore right?

In this chapter I will break down the various types of dangers that can cause our thoughts to shift away from pursuing our hopes and dreams. We will see how through our daily decision-making and ways of thinking about our self and our circumstances can affect our personal growth, and most importantly our progress, along the journey to our destiny. So let's take a look at a few dangers that we encounter every day.

Perception

We can get so caught up in the lives of others. Their success, relationships, and notoriety can so consume your thoughts that you stop truly living your own life from getting bogged down into theirs. We follow the rich, the not-so-rich, the famous, the "wannabe" famous on Twitter, Facebook, YouTube, Instagram and more. We have TMZ, Entertainment Tonight, 24-hour news and information. There is way too much access to way too many people. There are folks who stay connected to this barrage of information day and night and never invest in their own lives. Their families go without their time and attention; their lives go without direction or passion and they become totally consumed in what they "believe" is a more beautiful and valuable life. Their perception of what is truly important in life is all off.

You may want what you see, but you have no clue as to what the other person did or suffered or paid to get there. With the multitude of unreal reality television shows, you don't even know for sure if this fabulous life is even their own! This faulty belief makes perceptions so dangerous because it can lead you into buying into all of the lies and deceit. You start walking down a path that is not your own and become lost within your own reality.

How do you deal with the danger of a perception? You can start by seeing and knowing the truth about a given situation. Do not let what you see, attract your thoughts. Don't let the fake and phony world draw you in. Do not put so much energy in keeping up with the people around you and make it your business to *live for you instead*! God created a specific destiny for you, a specific journey for you, do not let the things you *perceive* to be important or valuable or desirable deter you from your journey.

We see and we want what we see. Our appetites can get the better of us. We believe that if we only obtain "those shoes or that car" that others will perceive that we are always in style or have a lot of money. God made all of us special and unique; not for us to walk around looking, dressing and acting the same.

Why is one man happy while another is miserable? Why is this person fearful and anxious while another is full of faith and confidence? Why does one person have a beautiful and luxurious home full of drama and trauma, while another who is driving a "paid for" hoopty (Yes, I said hoopty) live full of gratitude, peace and contentment in a small rental apartment? (And notice that I did not say that the man with the small apartment is "poor," because it's all perception anyway). Perception, that is why! If you believe that you are blessed then you will see yourself as such. When you discover the truth about your situation and even that of others, you can conquer the danger of perception. The answer to all these questions is found deep within our subconscious mind. Whatever we constantly think, talk and feel about ourselves will ultimately become a reality. These thoughts will register in the subconscious mind as beliefs. This means, if a person constantly feels he is unlucky and a big failure in life, is likely to *become* one in all his endeavors. And the good news is that you can "think" your way to success, joy and gratitude. You can look to your future with great anticipation and most importantly, focus on what you can do to make it real. You stop living in someone else's life and begin to truly "live" in your own!

Do you believe that if you speak success into the atmosphere that success will come? Well, I believe it 100 percent, but let me just make one thing clear, that's not all you have to do! You have to learn how to escape the dangers of the mind.

In my early lived life I have found that my mind can in fact play tricks on me. I can get caught up in going out, always being on the scene and attending numerous promotional, political and social events. This is not to say that being out and about is bad but making sure that we choose wisely on where we spend our time, money and energy is critical. Sometimes what started as a nice networking opportunity can turn into a big waste of time. I'm not ashamed that once upon a time I felt that I needed to be everywhere all the time; but I share this with you because it's all about promoting growth and learning from youthful mistakes.

Fear

In today's society, fear is HUGE because it is such a very common danger to our mind. As I see it, fear is just another excuse not to progress in life. A popular acronym for the word fear is **F**alse **E**vidence **A**ppearing **R**eal. Why do you think many people are fearful? Are they scared of failure? Are they afraid to be different? Fear can be a serious stumbling block to your success! Fear is why some people have not become millionaires, are unable to make their own schedules *and* why many people are living meaningless, mediocre lives.

My life is an open book and I try to turn most of my experiences into a life lesson for myself or others. For example, if you have to take a big test in order to gain a higher level of certification, you should not question yourself or worry about what will happen. If you have prepared and worked hard the problem is all in your mind because you are questioning your abilities. When you are confident and know who you are and where you are going then no person, place or thing should be able to deter you. God often times sends us tests or trials that we must pass in order to reach a certain level in our maturity! These tests are not to deter us from the ultimate goal or dream in life, but they are to build us up to be stronger and wiser which allows us to walk confidently towards our destiny.

When Fear comes your way you have to continually remind yourself that you are part of some larger purpose or plan and that you can't let yourself down.

I've never been a person too scared to just risk it all. That may sound crazy and often times, I think I am (Smiles)! Sometime it costs me but I always come away with something as a result, either a victory or a valuable life lesson.

Fear often allows us to deal with the uncertainty in knowing. God does not reveal all his plans for our lives at one time, so just like jumping rope in Double-Dutch, there will be sometimes where you are outside of the action, trying to figure out your timing and rhythm to jump in! In other words outside of the loop is always uncertainty but if you trust in yourself, your worth, and your dream then no uncertainty, no FEAR can get the victory.

Brokenness

All brokenness is not bad, but when it interferes with your progress, then something is wrong. I walked around broken for a long time. Brokenness can stem from childhood issues that remain with you into adulthood. For example, I habitually chose bad boys for relationships who would end up breaking my heart. To the point that when I started meeting good men, that I would never really open up and allow them the opportunity to know the *real* Kristen because my heart was so cold from the past.

I would run away from or sabotage anything that even hinted of a relationship. I wouldn't allow people to know too much about me, I didn't like to expose who I was or let them get too close. This caused me to go down a dangerous path where I didn't care about me, you or anyone else. I didn't care about their feelings or their hearts. I would be so heartless when it came to men to the point where it became a huge distraction in my life. I would drop what I was doing to go to dinner with a man, even though majority of the times I wasn't focused on the situation or would eventually lose interest. I only did it to entertain myself or for whatever benefits I could get out of it.

When you are that broken, you don't think clearly, especially once it has become a cycle that you relive over and over again. Once there was a man who disrespected me to the point that I truly wanted to HURT him! He embarrassed me over and over again by his actions and by *my* inaction I embarrassed *myself* by taking it! This is when I sat down and analyzed the situation. He felt he could act that way because of the way I presented myself. I always acted cold and heartless so he figured that I wouldn't or couldn't be hurt from his behavior. I realized that being cold and heartless not only devalued others, but it devalued me as well. What a revelation! From that day forward, I promised myself that I would never settle for just anything or devalue my worth for anyone.

Once I eliminated that mindset, I knew I would be greater than I was, and when the right person came along I would know, be ready to embrace him and allow him into my life and heart.

One thing I've learned for sure is that no matter what happens, life keeps going. Time waits for no man. When most of us finally get this, we begin to live, and keep living *on purpose*! Even through hard times and trials, all we can do is live, but what about the times of heartache and pain that we have not fully over come? Where does it go? Do we place it on the backburner and act like it doesn't exist? Do we carry the dead weight on our shoulders until we become tired? What happens is that brokenness becomes yet another dangerous thought that hides away in the back of your mind waiting for the right (or wrong) situation to arise. Before you know it you have derailed your dreams -- *again*.

We can't move forward in life or find true happiness if we are broken inside. I know you would rather be strong. You believe that if you don't allow yourself to think on it that it would just fade away. But to tell the truth, it will only fade away for a season only to show up as trust or anger issues, abuse, co-dependency or another dysfunctional relationship.

When we acknowledge our broken places, thinking or actions and decide to work toward the healing process we won't run to the familiar places within our *brokenness* every time a tough situation appears. We must change our mindset to be delivered and set free from it once and for all.

The 3 D's

When it comes to dangers of the mind here are **3 D's** to consider:

1. *Distressed*- When you are so worried that you don't put enough time and energy into your own vision or work.

2. *Distracted*- When we believe that we have found ourselves in the right place at the right time but discover that we are in fact *all wrong*. As I discussed earlier you don't have to be at EVERY party, go on EVERY trip and attend EVERY concert. There are some things you have to sacrifice for the happiness to come in the end. Sometimes there are other priorities that require our full attention.

3. *Dependent*- When we start depending on others to provide, whether it's to pay a simple bill, or to always have our back and bail us out of trouble, we become, say this word with me... COMPLACENCY! This word is a VERY scary term for me! I NEVER want to be complacent ever again in life. I had to take responsibility for my life and its direction. We all must be prepared to do the work.

Complacency

A little more about complacency -- it is being satisfied with how things are and not wanting to make them better.

People that have remained at a job for years, and have not been elevated in their careers have become complacent. You don't desire more, you don't do more, and you don't even feel that you deserve more. Life is all about progress – moving forward and you can't do so if you are too busy being comfortable in your daily situations. Often times, we get to a place of satisfaction, and don't get me wrong, it's okay to be happy about your accomplishments and have some degree of satisfaction with your life, but you should not get so comfortable that you become old news with nothing new to talk about. Complacency can lull your mind into a deep sleep, but in order to be greater in everything that you do, you must *want* to achieve more. That, dear friends, is the answer to complacency, it is known as passion!

It all began in late 2009 and here I am, graduating from college during a recession with no job prospects lined up. "THINK like a BOSS, ACT like a BOSS" was NOT my mindset. However, once you discover that you possess certain talents or skills and your mind allows you to think in terms way beyond your years, it can be a true blessing. But sometimes thinking beyond your years will lead you to *act* beyond your years making things a little uncomfortable for you among your peers. This is not to say that it comes naturally for everybody but I had no problem taking a few leaps of faith. And not to discredit or put down any of my past, current or future friends -- but when your mind is set up differently, you see the light at the end of the tunnel shinning a little brighter than the next guy. This doesn't mean that you are better than them; it just means that you have received clarity on your vision earlier than most and are ready to get up and go for it.

When you have a vision, what do most ambitious people want to do? Create it, right? Develop it, nurture it, and watch it grow. Then there are *some* people who take the opposite approach and procrastinate, look for hand-outs, excuses and do not develop a hustler's mentality.

It was tough for me at first because I was different and for my age, way ahead of the game. At 22 I was doing Public Relations work for one of the top advertising firms in Connecticut. I already had a five-bedroom house that my parents allowed me to use when they moved to North Carolina, AND I was running a Public Relations company of my own on the side. You would think that I would start working my plan and firming up my strong foundation. But no, complacency had set in. I was making a decent amount of money but instead of putting the majority of my time into building my business, I devoted only 10-12 hours a week. The rest of the time was PARTY TIME! I went on TONS of trips with my friends, went to TONS of events, and even threw a HOUSE party or two.

I saw myself as young, large and in charge with NO rules, no limits. After all I had it going on. What more could I ask for? What I should have asked for was a mentor, a growth plan, a savings plan, some passion. What I got was COMPLACENT! Even until this day the word brings fear and dread to my heart! I will never, EVER be complacent again! This phase of complacency lasted for over two years. Don't get me wrong, it didn't mean that I wasn't getting things done; I just could have done MORE. I wasn't growing and progressing the way I knew I could. I wasn't MAXIMIZING my OPPORTUNITIES and I certainly wasn't being the entrepreneur I could have been. I was living below my potential.

Complacency can make us get so wrapped up in our lives, that we really think we got it going on, but then you need to sit back and ponder what life is REALLY about? I had to ask myself this same question, and what I came up with was PROGRESS! Every year there is a new "must watch" celebrity on television or in social media. There is always a new "IT" person. Revolving leaders on the world stage shift and change from year to year, generation to generation.

Sometimes you get someone who stands the test of time and becomes an icon, a standard bearer. But most fade away, a subject on the next edition of "What ever happened to...?" This is what life is really about – a changing of the guard, seeing who rises to the top. In the world of complacency, if you are comfortable being average or with your station in life you make no room for growth and more room for error and ineffectiveness.

Insecurity

Everyone feels insecure at times, but some are better at managing this state of mind while others allow it to manage them, wearing it on their sleeves for all to see. **Insecurity** is when you are not secure or are full of anxiety about matters. These are sometimes things that we view as flaws, weaknesses, or problems with ourselves. The source of insecurities stem often from your thoughts. I always tell myself I am my own worst critic. I judge myself really harshly in an effort to make myself do better. Often times we can judge ourselves so harshly that we begin training our minds to be insecure in a specific area such as our looks or living conditions. We must learn not to allow insecurity to take us down but look at it optimistically as an opportunity to create an environment for change and lift us up.

I become a little perplexed by how much insecurity can change the direction of your life. How many more successes would we have experienced, how many more endeavors would we have tried if we were more secure in who we are and what we can accomplish? When I first started writing this book I felt that I was always pretty confident in myself. No real insecurities to think of, but God led me to take a second look at my thinking and I began to really analyze my life and thought back to my early success with the big advertising firm in Connecticut. When I started for almost a year I was the youngest as well as the only African American person working for the company. At a very young age I quickly began to understand corporate America. I will admit that I was uncomfortable to the point of lacking confidence in what I could offer at the table. There were times in meetings where inappropriate jokes or comments were made while I sat there among them and I didn't feel confident to address them on the spot. Unfortunately I didn't recognize my behavior back then as insecurity, but now I see it was.

Holding onto insecurities can cause you not to succeed in ways that you know you can. Insecurity will cause you to act in ways that are not authentic. There were times when I doubted myself even when I KNEW I was intelligent, capable and a hard worker. I don't believe that I ever went as far as to purposely hurt anyone because of my insecurities, but there is an old saying that says, "hurt people, (will) hurt people" and that is certainly a very dangerous state of mind to be in.

Ego and Pride

The ego can cause you to act and think rather selfishly. You must get yourself in a place of humility and take some time to work on the things you have *not* done yet. When I started surrounding myself around with older entrepreneurs that have been in business for years, I did not want to take time and boast on my accomplishments, I wanted to spend more time, trying to learn and grow so that I can gain new achievements.

Now on the other hand, some of us have bigger heads driven by egos which secretly feed on our insecurities (but we can act like I didn't say that). Some of us, if we can see how big our heads have become, wouldn't be able to move because of the sheer weight of it. Ego and Pride often go hand in hand but sometimes your pride can cause you to miss your blessing. I have missed out on plenty of opportunities because I wasn't as transparent as I should have been and it was nothing but my pride standing in the way. Pride continues to play a huge factor in my life and I admit that I am still being delivered from its effects. I refuse to let people know when I'm hurting, when I'm struggling, when I'm down or distressed, etc. This was something I had to give to God and pray about concerning the shaping of my character and to help me not to allow my ego to get in the way, especially when I know that I need to work on it. In order to grow stronger in my character pride must loosen its grip on my thinking – even it if is just a little bit at a time.

In this chapter we touched on Fear, Perception, Brokenness, the 3D's (Distressed, Distractions, and Dependent) Complacency, Insecurities, Ego and Pride. These are very common dangers of the mind that can lead you to a heart full of pain, and a life without passion or direction. I have been there in each place and found it to be a dangerous world for me.

What dangerous perceptions have you held in the past? How did they affect your life?

Has there been a time when your ego or your fears blocked your progress? If so, in what ways has it done so?

Have you been able to recognize the 3 D's at work in your life? If so, what did you do? If not, what should you have done?

Affirmation – Think about what you have learned in this chapter and jot down 3 things to remember the next time a" Danger of the Mind" blocks your progress:

1.

2.

3.

Chapter 2

Breaking the Chains of Distractions

What does the word *distraction* mean? It is anything that prevents someone from giving their full attention to something else. *Aha!* And when you don't give your full attention to your goals, objectives or your dream, you end up WASTING CRITICAL TIME!

Let's take a few moments to think about some common distractions. What comes to mind? Are there specific people, places or things? Are you a TV junkie? (Just a side note, reality TV can be a good thing, but remember *they* are getting paid for sharing how they moved from just *dreaming* their dreams to *living* them. So don't get so caught up in watching that you begin to neglect the business of moving and getting things done in your *own* reality!)

For months and months I set expectations and goals but I rarely got what I wanted or needed accomplished. I knew each item on the list was achievable but when I looked at why I wasn't making progress and I found a cold, hard truth. Distractions!

You cannot expect to meet even the most reasonable expectations if you don't work to eliminate or at least control distractions in your daily life. The process of dealing with distractions starts with us. We must realize when we are allowing the distraction to continue to control our lives. For example, it can start by simply going in to check your Instagram account at the start of your day. Let's say it's 9:00 a.m. when you get started and before you know it you are still on-line, "Liking" photos, offering a few LOLs and suddenly it is 9:30! You throw in "Liking" 20 or so motivational posts but you fail to actually get motivated into doing some work on your own life. Then the distraction continues as you move onto Twitter and then Facebook. Next you are responding to a text from a friend about what happened the *night before*. So now you're texting away about the *past*. What time is it now? Take a wild guess. YES, it's now 10:30! Another hour has gone by, and your computer monitor is not even hot yet.

In a sense technology has made our lives much easier, but it has also made it harder for us to escape something or someone. There are multiple ways to get in touch with someone now. If you can't get them on a text or phone call, you can try email, Twitter, or Facebook. Oh and let's not see that they posted something on Instagram, after *not* responding to your efforts to get hold of them! So we must be careful with social media not only because it's so accessible to us, but it makes us too accessible to *others*. We can get so caught up in the lives that others are living that we stop living our own.

There are so many distractions that can slowly KILL our dreams without our even knowing it. The one character trait that I have and pray that I hold on to is not to judge others when it comes to their mistakes or certain lifestyles. Everyone has skeletons in their closets and a certain way they would like to be perceived. They also have regrets and choices they would like to have a second chance at making. And one such situation that I see affecting this generation among other generations in the past is our "if only" moments.

How many times have we heard, "If only I had been just a little more careful..." "If only I didn't have one more drink of liquor," "If only I would have just stayed home." "If only, if only, if only...!" Someone once said that, "setbacks are just set ups for something greater!" So if you or someone you know finds yourself struggling to get over an "if only" situation then I have good news for you. It's not over! Your dreams are still alive and you can still achieve far above and beyond your wildest imagination!

> *Setbacks are just set ups for something greater!*

There a many types of distractions and some are certainly more harmful than others. One type can be found in pursuing random sexual encounters. I encourage you to ask yourself if your significant other, boyfriend, girlfriend, side piece, *shawty*, lover, or WHATEVER you want to call them, are speaking success into your life? Are they lifting you up to be a better person? If you told them you can't go out tonight because you have to work or study, would they cut you off, or not want to be around you anymore? Will they offer ultimatums or understanding? Having a companion or a soul mate is a wonderful thing in anyone's life, if they are the *right* one. But having the *wrong* one can KILL your dreams! Choose wisely and be confident in your choice and make sure that you are the right person for them. You should uplift, support and offer understanding in return. Remember that you reap what you sow. Be there for them and be their #1 fan! If you have chosen well, you will have a #1 fan in your corner in return.

Distractions can become a part of your daily life. Any and everyone that knows me, know that I have my phones (yes, I said *phones*) with me WHEREVER I go. Many of my calls are business-related, but to tell the truth many of my entrepreneurial friends are counted among my personal calls throughout the day as well. I have gotten MUCH better at managing these calls because I have learned that my phone had become one of my biggest distractions. One method that I use is to let most calls go to my voicemail. I typically end my day around 6:00 p.m. or later so my voicemail message tells the caller that I will check all messages after 7:00 p.m. and will get back with them accordingly. Time management strategies such as these are very important to any entrepreneur and you should think about using them to control distractions as well.

Another time management strategy I have is to setting aside time for certain tasks throughout my day. For example, I have set aside 2 hours for writing but if I kill 30-45 minutes on an unexpected phone call I must now shift or eliminate other items on my agenda for the day.

The beauty of being an entrepreneur is that you don't have to punch the clock for **anybody** which gives you a lot of flexibility in how you spend your time. BUT that perk comes with responsibilities. You have to be VERY disciplined and prepared to work longer hours than the normal 9-to-5. This flexibility also makes it easier for friends to call you and convince you to come have a drink, eat meals at unconventional hours and chit-chat about life and love. And even though we all need some down time and must attend to our relationships we must still be careful not to allow these sweet moments to become distractions as well. Self-control comes into play when we are seeking to become disciplined in managing our time.

When Distractions Can Become Dangerous

On February 23, 2013 I was driving home one night about 4:00 a.m. It was during a torrential down pour but, for some odd reason I insisted to my friends that I could make it home safely. After all, I lived only 5 minutes away, but I had been drinking.

I started to drive and couldn't see that clearly because of the rain. I approached a corner, one that I manage to negotiate almost every single day. When I saw the huge pool of water my first reaction was to stop but when I hit the brakes, I hydroplaned and the water took full control of my car! According to a witness on the scene I spun around about 7 times and ended up striking a metal pole. Now this was happening *while I was on speaker phone* with a friend. The phone was in my lap. Once I opened my eyes after impact, in a panic I began to move the airbag out the way. I could see in the distance people running up to my car. With the debris from the air bags burning my face, I managed to open the

32

door and stumble out the car. The first person to reach me was a taxi driver named Manny.

Manny very gently assessed my condition and yelled out to onlookers, ""She's alive, she's ok". At this point I was still very confused and my head was pounding. I turned to look at my car it was nearly wrapped around the pole! I began to cry hysterically and Manny walked me over to his taxi and sits me down until the police arrive on the scene. When the police arrive, the officer looks at the wreckage and asks "is this your vehicle?" I answered yes, and then he says, "Well I don't know who is watching over you, but from the looks of your car, you are not supposed to be here." Manny the taxi driver even went off of his route to drive me to my house. God bless him.

I was terribly traumatized for nearly 2 weeks after that incident. I didn't eat for the first two days. The next day I went to the hospital by myself and sat in the emergency room, just praying. My head was hurting so bad, that I thought I was going to die right there in that room. The CAT scan and other tests came back and the doctor reported that I was perfectly fine. Other than the effects of the airbag burning my face for another couple of weeks, God allowed me to walk away from that situation without a scratch.

Not even two month later, on April 15th I experienced another huge distraction. I was in my bathroom getting ready for my friend Katrina's cookout. I was so excited to get over there, because another one of my good friends had come to Atlanta to visit. Suddenly, I hear water dripping, and at first I thought it was my dog King, sipping out of his bowl. As the sound continued, I walked out into the hallway where I see water pouring out of the light fixture. I'm in shock at this point, so when I hear more water in another part of the unit, I run down the hall, only to see more water gushing from the ceiling of the second bathroom, near my living room. I turn again and see water coming out of the kitchen sprinklers.

I now come to the realization that my place is about to be flooded so I grab my dog while I am trying to gather up what valuables I could off the floors and put them up onto higher surfaces. Now the building contains privately-owned condos and since this was a Saturday it was next to impossible to get someone to respond quickly and contain the problem. I ran up the stairs to see the source of the water. I run to the unit over mine and start banging on the door. No one seems to be there, but water is running out from under the door. I realize that I left my phone on the bed so as I am heading back to my place I see the owner of the other unit. He tells me he was trying to put in a vanity and burst the pipes. Two hours later my neighbors are helping me put some of my stuff safely away and there is still no sign of building maintenance.

Now a few weeks after that incident, I wake up early, motivated and ready to start my day. I turned on my 3-year old computer for a regular day of work when the indicator light flashes on, flickers and then goes off. After trying repeatedly to get it started, I take it to Best Buy for service. It turns out that my computer is completely fried.

I could go on and on but I share these three specific stories that occurred over a 4 month period. Each incident involved major aspects of my life -- my transportation, my home, a critical resource for my work and almost cost me my very life and limb.

I am a strong person. I kept fighting and I kept going and I would not allow any of those trials to get the best of me. Some things I feel I did right. I thanked God for His grace and mercy. I didn't become fearful so I kept going out, having fun, and tried making better decisions. What I didn't realize then, but I know now is that God was trying to tell me to be still and know that He has equipped me with everything I need to make it through.

Often God allows things to be taken from us, to show us *who* we are and what we are made of. Sometimes it is to teach us how to stand on His promises and depend on Him to supply our needs, to protect us and to keep us sane. I walked away from that accident without a scratch. God was showing me

that if He could bring me out of that situation when I didn't
have the faith or sense to trust in Him then imagine how great
my life would be once I did?

Don't run from your problems and absorb yourself into the lives of others. These are the times when distractions can often be the most LOUD and uncontrollable. The decisions you make will cost you something in the long run. You have to pay to play in this game of life. You must pay attention to all of the things happening around you. Don't be so caught up in trying to maintain the things that are not important and not take the time to reflect on the lessons you need to learn in order to grow from each trial.

Now that you have some significant examples from my life, let's walk through the steps of **breaking the chains of distractions**! I want you to literally picture breaking chains off of you. I want you to feel the cold steel, the weight, and the rough edges cutting your skin. Why? Because this is how agonizing some hurts and pain are in real life. To be consumed by distractions can become a terrible habit. Some people major in being distracted and continuously see themselves as victims. I could have easily given in to my circumstances and cried "Poor me, feel sorry for me, why me?" It is not easy to break a habit but I know that you are stronger than that and that you can do it! So whenever you encounter a potentially destructive distraction:

1. **Acknowledge your distractions.**

   Take a look around your life and see what your main distractions are and what you can do about them. Assess your part in the problem. Is it establishing time management principals, making better choices or wiser decisions? What keeps holding you back from accomplishing some goals and objectives?

2. **Understand your surroundings.**

   Take an inventory of your circle of influence. Who is truly around you to build you up and make you better? Who is there only to create negative energy, drama and suck the life out of you? Who is just taking up space? Are they a fan? Are *you* a fan of theirs? Start cutting loose certain people, situations and mindsets!

3. **Tear the distraction apart, piece by piece.**

   What are the lessons? What are you supposed to learn about yourself, others or even God in this distraction? Are you going to grow from this or are you going to wallow in it?

4. **Choose to deal with distractions.**

   This is the most important part. Once you make the decision to break the chains of distractions, you have to move forward in confidence and with clarity that you made the right decision. Once you break away from people, places, thinking and behaviors; don't go back! It is tempting and so easy to fall back into old habits. Practice self-leadership and remind yourself daily of your goals, your dreams and your objectives. Remember why you made a critical move to pursue your dreams in the first place.

5. ***Remember that everybody is not on your side.*** One thing that I learned is when you are doing something good and especially something that is good for *you*, everybody is not going to be sincerely happy for you. That's just life. When you believe in a dream and you want to make it a reality you HAVE to eliminate as many distractions as you can.

Don't let distraction be your comforter, don't let distraction be your go-to man, don't let distraction become your resting place because it seems easier than fighting or dealing with life. Eliminate the distractions by facing your problems and making the decision to grow through it. So I say to you let go of those daily distractions because they can lead to dangerous situations that can kill your spirit, your motivation, your strength to fight and ultimately your dreams.

As part of this chapter's "Closing Thoughts," you were cautioned to **Understand Your Surroundings**. Are you beginning to re-think some of the people in your circle of influence? Are there some you should drop; or add? Who and why?

Affirmation – Think about what you have learned in this chapter and jot down 3 actions you can take:

1. Now –

2. **Within the next 30 days –**

3. **Within the next 6 months –**

Chapter 3

Recreating the Atmosphere

In the process of eliminating your distractions, you will come to a place where you can choose to recreate your atmosphere. How is that done? Well, it may be a decision that you must come to terms with. It could be that you are forced to change your environment in order to survive. Some situations are more critical than others. Read on while I clarify what I mean.

In the last chapter I touched on distractions. In that time in my life, it was part of God's plan to prepare me for restoration. He began to rebuild and restore everything that I had lost. This shift in the atmosphere was due to my making a decision to push past my circumstances. I decided to keep going toward my destiny. I let some negative things go and embraced some others that empowered, encouraged and elevated my thinking. This chapter will discuss this process and how it has come to play a major role in my successes and my progress.

When you set your mind on pursuing your dreams, it should be such a beautiful time in your life. You find that as you focus on eliminating distractions and commit to meeting your goals and objectives you will gain an internal peace about your future no matter what is going on around you.

I absolutely live by this acronym for PEACE; Positive Energy Activates Constant Elevation! In a previous chapter I mentioned how critical it is to be surrounded by positive people. If you don't have the right people in your circle you cannot expect growth and prosperity to be your destiny. My mother always told me that *if you hang around nine poor people you are going to become the 10th poor person.* So it seems it would stand to reason that if you hang around *nine rich people,...* yeah you got it! Seems easy enough, right? NOT! I'm afraid that there are some people in your life that you love and adore who have been around for years and yet are not necessarily counted among the "rich" people. And don't get me wrong, I'm not talking about being rich financially, but in terms of their mentality and how they think and live and relate to others.

WISE people can make your vision so much clearer. Their conversation, their attitude and positive energy all add up to a rich outcome. The atmosphere you live in can make or break you. Being around intelligent and wise people can condition your mind to think like them and become successful like them in return.

Recreating your atmosphere is a process. I said earlier in the book that it takes about seventeen days to break a habit. However, the process took me longer because I was stuck in some of my ways. God soon revealed to me, that He couldn't take me to a new place in my life, if I held on to my old habits and behaviors.

For example, I found that my diet was unhealthy and served only to weigh me down. The sluggishness I suffered as a result affected both my body and mind. So in effort to recreate my atmosphere I learned that there are actually foods that make you operate better. Glucose is fuel for your body and it keeps your brain clear and alert. It not only keeps us functioning daily but inevitably it affects the way you think, feel and work. Why do you think that you are so tired after eating a plate of good old soul food? Why does your productivity go way down after big lunch or even dinner? It is because of foods that are full of unhealthy amounts of sugars, fats and other ingredients that work to weigh you down with a serious need for a nap.

Recreating your atmosphere takes a lot of hard work but remember that the stronger you are in your resolve to do and be better, then the more control you have over your thought life. And better thoughts, mean a better life!

We all need affirmation. Speak words of power and positivity into your circumstances. Focus your mind, solely on what you are doing and what you need to do. It is critical to remember that no matter how busy you are, you must make time for yourself. Even if it is only 30 minutes a day, this time must be devoted to self-care. If you give yourself the luxury of <u>free time</u> then you will find that meeting the rest of your responsibilities get easier. We need to step away from being in the trenches, even if it is from something we are passionate about to stay fresh and focused.

Three practices that I find are critical to this process of recreating your atmosphere are to pursue your peace; find your purpose and find your journey.

1. *Pursue Your Peace*

    Self-peace not only keeps your spirits up and drama free but also creates a fruitful place for self-love to form. It is in your peaceful times that you should find silence. Don't be afraid of that silence. All my life I loved to be around people. I usually have someone to accompany me on shopping trips, travel, running errands or to events. When I got my own place, even though I lived alone, I never felt alone because there was always someone dropping by, friends, companions, or family members. Always!

So when recreating my atmosphere I embraced my quiet time and this created peace within. It was something I never experienced before and I absolutely loved it. My quiet time is where some of my best ideas formed. In your quiet time you can pray, meditate, read, or write. It's a time to establish a launching pad for your next move, a time to focus on you and no one else.

If practiced regularly, the effects of the peace created in this atmosphere will carry you through the tests and trials of your daily life. Your character will take shape and soon bring peace to others. The Bible says that a calm answer turns away wrath. You will find that others will be in a more peaceful state just by being in your presence.

With peace comes balance. Balance is a huge part of the atmosphere you want to maintain around you. You need to know how to balance everything on your plate whether you're a parent or a student in full time employment. Take the time to practice cultivating self-peace, it will put life into perspective and help bring order and balance into your world.

2. *Find Your Purpose*

One of the most critical *and* most beautiful times in your life is when you find your purpose. I know that I am placed on this earth to help connect people. I am not in the field of Public Relations by mistake, but God revealed to me that the field of public relations is much bigger than my eyes can see. If I had not taken the time to recreate my atmosphere I never would have known or understood the true meaning of building a foundation.

It's easy to get caught up in following the destinies of others and then lose sight of your own in the process. If you are reading this and feel like you are lost right now – take hope – because it's never too late to turn your life around and live for you.   Once you find your purpose that is not all you will find. You find your heart's desires. You start to truly understand your destiny and joys, pains and gains along the way to this wonderful discovery. Life is much more meaningful and beautiful when you are living it with purpose.

3. *Embrace Your Journey*

Living a life of peace and purpose is all about embracing your journey. I can often times be very hard on myself by being my own worst critic. But when I recreated my atmosphere and put things into perspective, I started to look at where I have been and where I am today. Not only have I grown physically but I have grown spiritually. I have also grown wiser and stronger than ever. Have I made some messed up decisions in life? HELL, YES! Would I take them back? NO, because if I didn't make those decisions I wouldn't have learned the lessons that I'm sharing with you now.

Embracing the journey can be so hard when you don't know what's next or what direction you're going in. That's why it's so important to know your purpose and have an awareness that your destiny is always at hand. **When God shows you His plan for your life, you can't help but to walk confidently in the knowledge that there is a purpose for everything you have gone through.**

The journey also teaches you a very valuable lesson about knowing your self-worth. When you realize all that you have accomplished, then you realize what you are capable of enduring. All you need is a little reminder of your worth. When you place action behind your intentions you become unstoppable.

On this journey in life, you have to do things you never done and go to places you have never gone. When you recreate your atmosphere, you're doing just that. You are stepping outside your comfort zone into the new, a place of fulfillment.

Recreating Your Atmosphere - Journal

Which of these strategies spoke to you the most and why?

___ Pursue Your Peace

___ Find Your Purpose

___ Embrace Your Journey

Affirmation – Think about what you have learned in this chapter and jot down 3 actions you can take on these strategies:

1. **Now –**

2. **Within the next 30 days –**

3. **Within the next 6 months –**

Chapter 4

Proclaiming Your Vision

A vision can never be lost once it is birthed within you. However, there are times when you might think that it has been "misplaced." God can always restore what you have lost. In life we tend to get stuck in the present time—struggling to look forward and not becoming the visionary that we are meant to be! We become so consumed with whatever is going on around and within us that we fail to see the bigger picture! Visualize success and what you want to accomplish. Whenever you lose focus think back to where the vision was clear. Revisiting those thoughts will help you to stay on track to bring your vision to reality.

Martin Luther King was a visionary. He was part of what you might call the Visionary Hall of Fame that includes the likes of Nelson Mandela, Oprah Winfrey, Steve Jobs, Debra Fox, Rosalind Brewer and the list goes on and on. Visionaries don't just wake up to a dream. They proclaim it in their walk and in their talk. They nurture it by absorbing information, investing time and money, cultivating relationships that add value and most of all, they *believe* in the vision.

This step of proclaiming your vision is the key foundation to having lasting success! Every idea needs to be visualized with some type of mental or physical image. I have friends who are great entrepreneurs and being a visionary is one thing that we all have in common. As you visualize your plan you become to know what it will look like at each stage of development. This knowledge will help you to know when you are on track and when you are wandering off the mark.

I have to admit, sometimes I tend to visualize too much and get excited and caught up on whatever place I am at the moment. It is easy to get fixated on the success of the moment and forget that there is more work to do. Just like an excited child on a road trip, we ask "are we there yet!" Well, when you are at the point of proclaiming your vision discernment should not be too far away. Discerning what's right for you, who's right for you, next steps, whose advice to take are all examples of exercising discernment.

I am still growing and maturing and yet I am still a dreamer. I dream almost every other night in my sleep, a sure sign that my mind is never at rest. My dreams would be so intense at times that I would wake up in a sweat because the dream seemed so real. Other times, my dreams would be so complicated that I would have to write them down in an attempt to make some sense out of it.

My mom shared with me that God speaks to us through our subconscious minds, ideas, visions and dreams. So now I definitely pay closer attention to all of my dreams.

There is a feeling of elation that comes from being a visionary and an entrepreneur that can become addictive. You start thinking you can do all things such as create an additional and equally profitable business while running another one. But you have to discipline yourself to stay on course. How many successful businesses suffered setbacks because they expanded their operations at the wrong time or without enough resources to make it work?

Proclaim what's yours and it shall be! I'm on the journey right along with you! I've seen it happen, not only in my life but in others. The exciting thing about this world is that we have the opportunity to create our own well-being. We have the freedom to create our own destinies.

No person or obstacle can keep you from your destiny if you walk with purpose.

Keeping your vision in front of you at all times, will help you proclaim your vision. And when you continue to move toward your vision, you start to see the vision with more clarity and focus. When you look at something long enough you begin to own it. Eventually it becomes such a part of your very being that you can't imagine living your life without fulfilling it.

When talking about vision, an often used Scripture is found in Proverbs 29:18a which reads: "Where there is no vision, the people perish..." (KJV). While it is not referring to the same kind of vision, the outcomes are similar. There is no sadder person in the world than one who is without hope. People without hope cannot see beyond their circumstances. They have a very limited view of life, love or success. They don't believe that it can happen for them. There is nothing but doom and gloom on the horizon and their dreams slowly shrink, fade away and die without ever realizing it's potential.

Don't allow hopelessness snuff out the vision for your life. Set standards that you believe in, set standards that you know only God can achieve. Do not limit yourself by the confines of your own mind. Your faith must be released into every aspect of your vision. Every time you see your vision, keep thanking him that it's on the way!

Success is a state of mind. If you want success, start thinking of yourself as a success! Once a vision is birthed, your creative imagination will soon take your heart captive! That is what passion is all about.

Your vision is just not for you! It impacts the lives of others. Whether you have a vision to be the world's greatest basketball player, the CEO of your own chain of hotels, or the one to find a cure for a devastating disease! Great visions are impacting people every day! Steve Jobs had a vision for a computer to be in every home in the world. Twenty years ago, who would envision a computer in your phone? Steve Jobs did! The longer you delay your vision, the longer it will take to impact others! So don't be selfish and limit your vision!

Proclaiming your vision is not just saying, "I've got a vision and it's only a matter of time and it's going to happen! You must place action behind it! You must prepare, sacrifice for it, talk about it and be about it!

I don't believe your vision can be as powerful as it's destined to be without trust in God or in yourself for the successful outcome of your endeavors.

God's dreams are far bigger than we can ever imagine for ourselves.

When proclaiming your vision, you began to develop the desire to see and make it happen. Really take time to develop the passion by getting motivated on a daily basis and being dedicated to your vision.

Be prepared for a bumpy road. There will be obstacles and setbacks. There will be challenges to overcome and some pain to endure. And certainly sometimes your vision will not appear like anything you ever pictured in your head. These road blocks are only meant for us to see a greater end! Anything worth having is worth fighting for and waiting for. The more it costs, the more we appreciate it!

No person or obstacle can keep you from your destiny if you walk with purpose.

Proclaiming Your Vision - Journal

Have you taken the time to put your vision to paper? If so, after reading this chapter which priorities do you plan to re-focus on your time and resources?

Affirmation – As you consider these priorities, jot down 3 actions you can take:

1. Now –

2. Within the next 30 days –

3. Within the next 6 months –

Vision Worksheet

Clarify your vision by answering the following 7 questions.

1. What are you passionate about (examples: education, community, youth, elderly, civic responsibility, financial freedom, entrepreneurship, etc.)

2. What are your gifts or skills? (They need to be attributes *others* have seen in you. In other words, if you *believe* you can sing and no one has ever asked you to do so?)

3. What job or task would you do for *free*?

4. What kind of daydreams do you have regarding your future? Do you see yourself on a stage, behind the scenes, in Congress, in a boardroom? Who else is there? What are they doing? What were you doing?

5. Where and when have you felt the most fulfilled? What gives you joy, satisfaction, a sense of excitement or accomplishment?

6. How do you spend your free time? Researching, reading, practicing, being out and about, watching people, seminars, parties, etc.?

7. What activities can you NOT get enough of? Talking about sports, sewing, cooking, writing, brain storming new ideas, organizing projects?

A Vision is a clear, challenging picture of the future you have for yourself. It will have the following components

1. It is influenced by your
    a.   values (what's important to you),
    b.   maturity (no childishness),
    c.   experiences (do you get out of your comfort zone, are you adventurous),
    d.   preparation (are you willing to sacrifice your resources to continue studying and training for it),
    e.   knowledge (do you know anything about the field),
    f.   skills, and
    g.   abilities.
2. It must be clear. (*when you share it, others can see it*)
3. It must be challenging. (*makes you stretch and grow*)
4. It must be a picture. (*you should be able to "see" it*)
5. It must have goals and objectives (*a plan*).

Goals must be SMART

1. **Specific** *(an artist vs a painter, etc.)*

2. **Measureable** *(a product; a clear idea of success, etc.).*

3. **Attainable** *(does it require education, funding, etc.)*

4. **Realistic** *(do you have the discipline, drive, courage)*

5. **Timely** *(deadlines, 30-day goal, 6-month goal, etc.)*

Write Your Vision

If you haven't done so already, you may consider this your 1st draft – just keep writing until you have identified all of the components of your *picture*. **Use "I" statements.** Then go back and edit it down to no more than two or three sentences. And don't put too much pressure on yourself. Your vision will grow and change along with your wisdom, knowledge and experiences. It will expand, grow and change as you meet and exceed each goal and objective on your journey!

Chapter 5

Preparing for Greater!!!!!!

I have addressed the Dangers of the Mind, Breaking the Chains of Distraction, Recreating Your Atmosphere and Proclaiming Your Vision. It's now time to prepare for GREATER!

This is an exciting time in your life, but if you are impatient it can be a frustrating one. After you have figured out how to manage your distractions, overcome obstacles, recreate your atmosphere and focus on your vision, it is only natural to get excited about your future. You have learned new skills, become engaged in the process, generated a passion for your destiny, but learning to wait is hard stuff. We all want to get to the finish line and the prize; however you have to embrace this part of the journey as well.

When we look into the definition of greater, it stems from the word great which by definition means "an amount or intensity considerably above normal or average." So when you read that definition out loud it's telling you that as you wait for your destiny to become your "here and now" and your vision to become reality, living your life becomes a time of preparation. You are getting prepared physically, emotionally, intellectually, and spiritually for a place or purpose that is considerably above the normal. After all, do you want a normal existence that anyone with a reasonable amount of effort can attain, or do you want a life that is above the norm? Don't you want a life that blows your mind and causes you to shake your head in amazement when you consider who you are, where you've been and what you've been through?

Every night for almost a year, I prayed faithfully for God to enlarge my territory. However, it seemed that I just wasn't getting anywhere. Nothing was changing and I finally asked God why I was not receiving the answer I wanted to that specific prayer. He did not answer me immediately but one day He revealed to me that in order for him to enlarge my territory I had to be *prepared* to receive it! Well, uh, duh!

You see, sometimes we want a certain lifestyle or mate or fortune and do not realize what others had to do to get them. Oftentimes, unless you are lucky enough to be exceptionally beautiful, wealthy or well-connected you don't realize how much work it takes to get those things. You must be prepared to work hard, have thick skin, and be disciplined. In addition you must be responsible, humble, grateful, and most of all you must maintain those character traits and more, even after you achieve your goals.

This season in your life is not going to be a breeze, because the greater can be so near yet feel so far away that you may feel like it will be a lifetime before it gets to you. This is a delicate time because there will be distractions; people, situations and other things that will try to bring you down or distract you from what you've learned along the journey. Keep in mind that you might be undergoing a testing of your faith or discipline just to see if you are ready to handle your success.

Honestly, I wasn't always the most disciplined person. I would fail and get back up, fail some more and try again. Then one day I recognized that these mistakes that I kept making over and over again where no longer mistakes, but were choices. In this life, you have to remain true to yourself and know that *you* are the only person blocking your progress and growth. The only person you are starving from the plate of success is yourself. No one's to blame, but yourself. After I stopped pointing the finger at others for my mistakes, I got up and did something about it. To quote the late, great mother of the people and poet extraordinaire Maya Angelou, "when you know better, you do better!"

Overtime, bumping your head against the same old brick wall is bound to get old and your wrong choices will start becoming the right ones. It's all about how you become ready to learn and grow and get into position to receive your greater. This next story is an example of how I came to recognize that a series of events were actually preparing me for *my greater.*

In the winter of 2008, I embarked on a journey that I knew would take me to great places. But what I didn't know was that it all was preparing me for something beyond my wildest dreams, *my greater.* Sometimes opportunities come and you have to jump at them. I was selected to go to Beijing, China and work for the 2008 Olympics. I was just a junior in college and had a boyfriend at the time, so the proposal was to spend 6 months out the country, learn mandarin and work for the Chinese Olympic News Service. The opportunity sounded great, but several questions began to crowd my thoughts. *"Months away from my boyfriend, family and friends? Going to a place where I didn't know anybody? Having to eat strange food and where most of the population spoke mandarin, a language that I can't even begin to decipher!"*

In the end I decided to go, not realizing until much later-that one decision would shape my life forever. That one decision would remind me time and time again to always think outside the box and not be afraid to make big leaps out of my comfort zone. From that day forward, that one decision led to other decisions that opened numerous doors for my career and made my future brighter than I could even imagine.

And the new experiences! The people I met and the places I visited were magical. The technology and how well advanced students were at my age was incredible. I met people from all over the world, many of whom spoke 5 or more languages!

Once I came back to the States, I wasn't even on campus for a semester before I was offered the opportunity to attend the prestigious Washington Center for a program which recruited students from all around the world engage in political forums and participate in outstanding internships. My boss, Scott Tribetz was a man that I would never forget. He owned Tricom Associates based in Arlington, VA. It is a PR firm whose client base is largely non-profit organizations and policy causes. The icing on the cake was that I lived in a high-rise condo in the affluent community of Bethesda, MD which is in suburbs of our nation's capital.

Despite the luxury living accommodations, it required that I commute by train an hour and a half each way, 5 days a week for 3 and a half months. But I was disciplined! I was never late and I used to stay after work to complete my school tests online, because I couldn't make it home in time. Mr. Tribetz was a great mentor and encourager. He would sometimes stay behind with me and help me with my tests. I didn't know but at this time, he was building my character and work ethic. I also got the opportunity to work with him on major events and projects, for example the video production of the merger between Delta and Northwest Airlines. Also I assisted at the International Association of Firefighters Convention with guest speaker, Vice President Joe Biden.

To end my internship, the Washington Center required us to find someone influential in the DC area. At the time, my long time good friend Chris Baker was picked up as a free agent by the Denver Broncos. He put me in touch with his sports agent, Chitta Malik, Senior Vice President for Football and Marketing at Perennial Sports & Entertainment. I conducted some research on Mr. Malik in order to write a paper and then sent it to him for his review and approval. He asked me to come in to meet him. My friend Candace, who lived in DC at the time, dropped me off at his office. Walking into the building, I didn't know that it would become another life-changing day. I sat down and had a great conversation with Chitta, he showed me around the office and introduced me to his business partner, Tony Paige. Tony was like a big teddy bear, he was so friendly and warm hearted. He asked what I was doing after college and I responded that at the time I had no clue. He began talking about how 2009 is the worst time to *find* a job because of the recession but he then uttered the words that changed my life. *"If you can't find a job, create your own."* I walked out of that office with my head held high feeling like the world was mine.

Soon after, I got together with a good friend of mine from college, Katrina Highsmith who also graduated with a Public Relations degree and talked to her about creating our own PR company. After further discussion, she decided that it was a great idea and in 2010 KH II Public Relations, LLC was born. Soon afterward we both got VERY good corporate jobs that we used to learn everything we could to better position and prepare ourselves in the Public Relations field.

Each of the internships that I worked while in college PREPARED me to work for the top rated advertising firm in Connecticut. This job led not only to gaining an immense amount of experience for my age, but also allowed me to meet influential people that would believe in me and help me along my journey. One such person became my mentor, Judy Young who owns and operates *six* McDonald's restaurants in Connecticut. I worked for the company for 2 years before resigning to relocate to Atlanta and pursue my entrepreneurial endeavors.

I take each experience that I have been though and hold it dear to my heart, because each experience was invaluable to my journey to the greater.

There comes a phase of the journey where you come to a crossroads. You must decide to go right or left, or wait. This can be a very exciting place because with each decision or choice, you can just feel the rewards and the taste of success getting closer with each step! But it's all in perfect timing! Your turn will come, and when it does, this stage of the journey (Preparing for Greater) has to be time well spent.

Can you think of some examples in your life where you prepared for something? How many times did you practice, recite something you needed to memorize, stood in the mirror and practiced your presentation?

That's preparing! In this stage you want to solidify, confirm and rededicate yourself to the vision if you have to. You must *know that you know* that when your dream awakes or when a key door opens up that you are ready and willing to start running towards it. Soon you are flying towards it and there is no looking back!

You are not getting caught in the traps of insecurities, perception, failures, or fear. The hurt and brokenness must be put behind you! This way none of the things that kept you

71

bound in the past will have control over you or your thoughts in the future, but instead you will keep your eyes on the greater!

I got the pleasure to meet an outstanding man by the name of Dr. Kingsley Fletcher also known as His Royal Majesty Drolor Bosso Adamtey, I. He is a world leader, author, educator, international advisor and the Suapolor (King) of SE (Shai) Traditional area in Ghana. I sat talking to him for many hours over several days. Just being in his presence gave me a sense of peace—it was a feeling that I never felt before. He had released a book entitled, "Who Says You Can't?" I decided to buy the book and ended up reading it every night for a month. This book profoundly changed my outlook on life. My favorite chapter was entitled, "Don't Waste Your Trials."

He says, "God wants to see the character that you will develop in the process of your trial so that when you come into his full blessing, you will be able to sustain the blessing rather than let the blessing destroy you." This was just so powerful to me, because at the time I was reading this book, I was experiencing what I felt to be one of the worst trials of my life. This passage let me understand that every trial and every situation that we go through is only preparing us for the greater, but while we are waiting for the greater there is still so much that needs to be done. We need to develop our character, because our character will shine the brightest during our greater moments.

The exciting part is not only *knowing* that your greater is coming, but being confident that your hard work is not in vain. There are four truths that you discover through your trials. To receive the ultimate victory you find that:

- *patience* is something you have to learn;
- *pain* is what you have to endure;
- *faith* is what you have to see;
- *responsibility* is what you have to take on!

Your greater is coming! Let's be clear, there are dangers ahead but there are actions you can take to ensure your success. There are distractions to deflect, perceptions to clear up and visions to proclaim. They involve making adjustments to your life and thinking. You must embrace your vision by being patient, passionate, perseverant, and prepared! You are on a journey, step out in faith and walk confidently towards your purpose.

YOUR GREATER IS COMING!

This chapter closes with four truths that you discover through your trials.

- *patience* is something you have to learn;
- *pain* is what you have to endure;
- *faith* is what you have to see;
- *responsibility* is what you have to take on!

Think of a time when you learned the greatest or most difficult life lesson and which of these truths was the result.

Affirmation – Now that you see these truths in a new light, what advice would you give someone going through a test or trial?

Continuing the Journey

This work is the foundation of a larger undertaking -- the launching of the **Dangers of the Mind** webpage! It will be a forum of help and healing not only for anyone facing tests and trials in their lives but a place that helps birth visions through stories. So many people live under their potential, under their circumstances. Part of my vision is to see **DOM** as a way to push and encourage others to higher heights! Visit www.Dangersofthemind.com and "Share your Story" on how you may have overcome a Danger of the Mind.

Feel free to drop us an email (info@dangersofthemind.com) or Tweet us (@Dangerofthemind). Like us on Facebook and Instagram (Dangersofthemind). I would love to take your questions and keep you abreast of my upcoming book tour and speaking schedule. Of course I hope that you will invite me to your book club or other groups to share **DOM** as well.

I look forward to hearing from you!

Made in the USA
Charleston, SC
20 June 2014